I Can Read About
SPIDERS

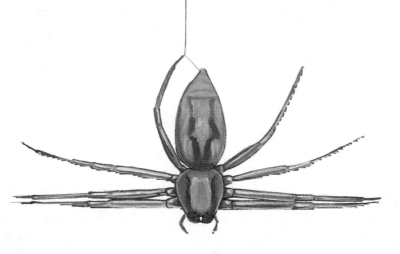

Written by Deborah Merrians • Illustrated by Kristin Kest

Troll

This edition published in 2001.
Illustrations copyright © 1997 by Kristin Kest.
Text copyright © 1997 by Troll Communications L.L.C.

Printed in the United States of America. ISBN 0-8167-4204-9

10 9 8 7 6

What's that scurrying in the grass? Is it a beetle or an ant? If you look closely, you'll see that it's a spider.

5

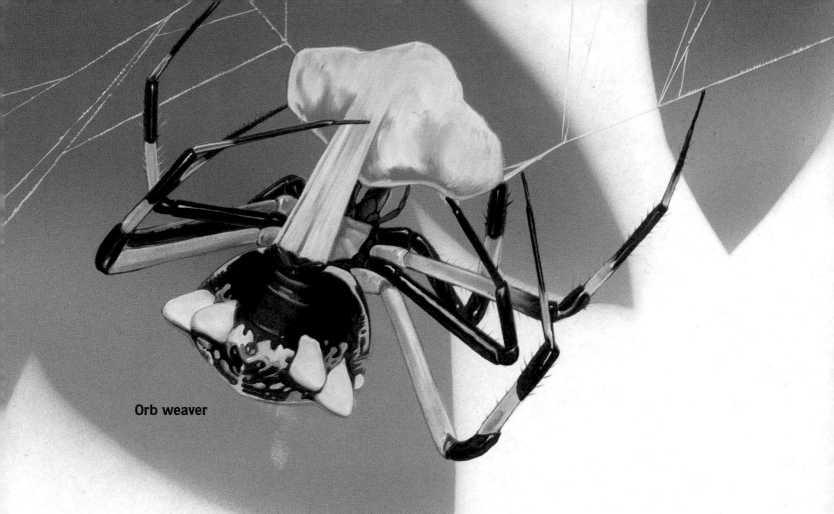
Orb weaver

Don't be afraid. Most spiders won't hurt you. In fact, the spider is one of our best friends in nature. That's because spiders love to eat insects. When they do, they eat many of the insects that are harmful to people.

Tick

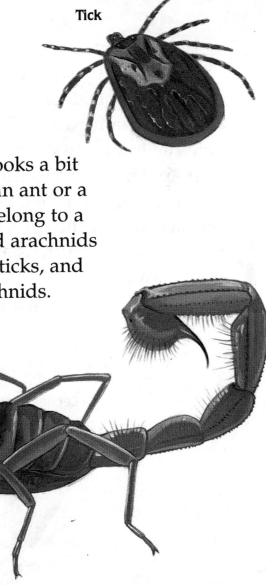

Mite

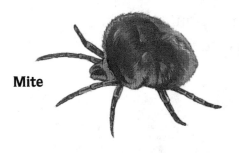

Although a spider looks a bit like an insect, such as an ant or a bee, it is not. Spiders belong to a group of animals called arachnids (a-RACK-nids). Mites, ticks, and scorpions are also arachnids.

Scorpion

7

How is a spider different from an insect? If an insect and a spider were set side by side, you could see many differences.

For example, look at this spider. It has eight legs and a body with only two main parts: a front part and a back part. The spider's head is in the front part of its body, which is called the cephalothorax.

A spider also has a thin shell, with tiny hairs covering its body.

Most spiders have eight eyes. And on each side of the spider's head, in front of its mouth, is a jaw with claws.

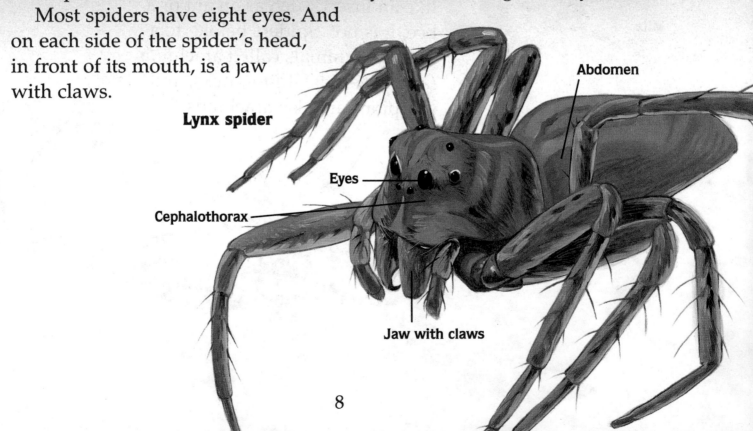

Lynx spider

Abdomen

Eyes

Cephalothorax

Jaw with claws

8

Now take a look at this insect. It has only six legs. Its body has three main parts: a head, a middle part, and a back part.

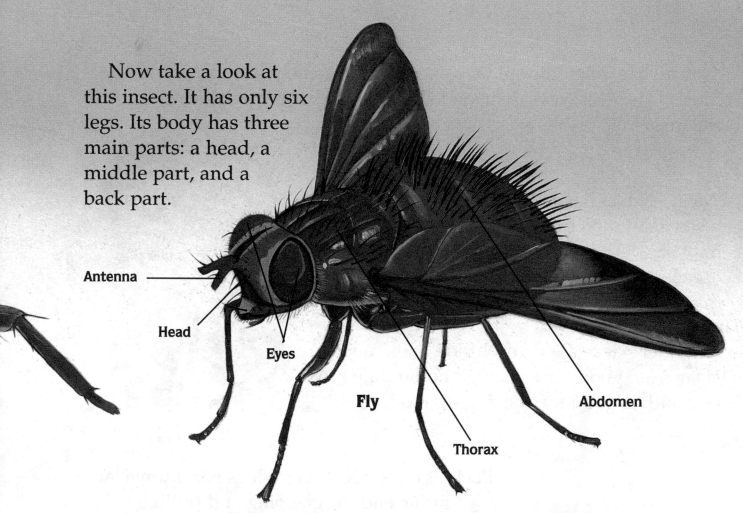

Antenna

Head

Eyes

Fly

Thorax

Abdomen

Many insects have wings. An insect also has a hard shell, as well as jointed legs.

On each side of the insect's head is a feeler called an antenna.

9

Nature has given the spider a special body to help it do its work. The spider's legs, eyes, jaws, hair, and abdomen all have special features. Here are some:

Eyes

Most spiders have eight eyes. Some spiders can see in all directions. But most spiders cannot see very well. Their eyes are used to sense changes in light.

Jaws

A spider has a jaw on each side of its mouth. The jaws are good for catching and holding food. The mouth is good for sucking up food.

Jaws

Claws

Legs

Each of the spider's eight legs has a tiny claw at the end for grasping and pulling. These claws also help the spider walk upside down without falling.

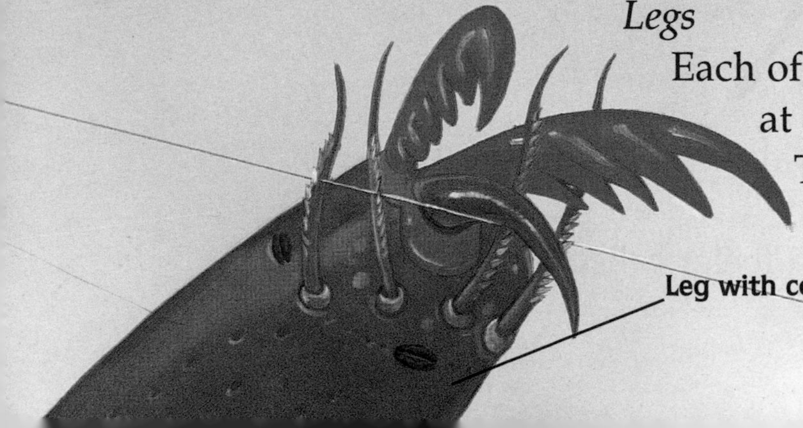

Leg with comb-feet and claw

10

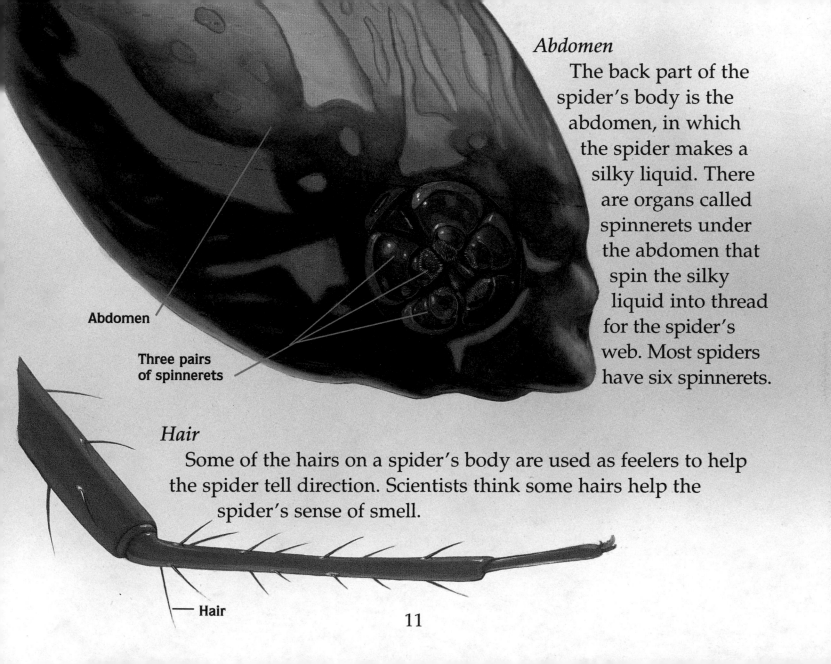

Abdomen

The back part of the spider's body is the abdomen, in which the spider makes a silky liquid. There are organs called spinnerets under the abdomen that spin the silky liquid into thread for the spider's web. Most spiders have six spinnerets.

Abdomen

Three pairs of spinnerets

Hair

Some of the hairs on a spider's body are used as feelers to help the spider tell direction. Scientists think some hairs help the spider's sense of smell.

Hair

11

Malaysian orb weaver

Spiders are amazing creatures! They can walk sideways, forward, backward, and upside down. They can also climb, carry things, run, jump, and swing.

Spiders are excellent hunters. They have many ways of catching their prey. Some spiders grab their victims with their jaws. Then the spider sucks up the insides of its prey with its mouth.

Other spiders spin silken webs in which to trap their enemies or prey. Spiders also spin silk for their homes and egg cocoons.

Crab spider

Alfalfa
butterfly

13

A spider may spin a different kind of silk for each job it does, making one type for a trap, another for a cocoon, and yet another for a home. This ogre-faced spider throws a web shaped like a net to catch its prey.

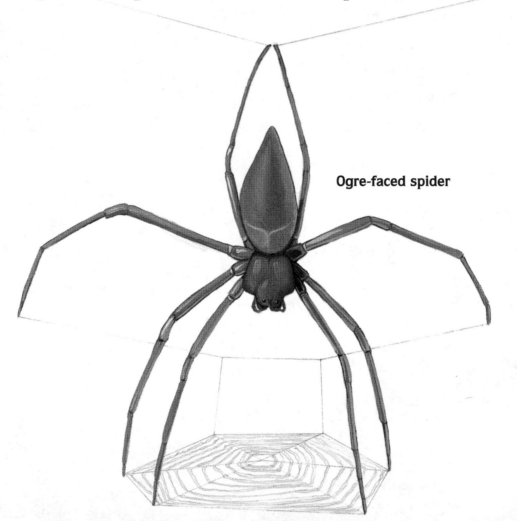

Ogre-faced spider

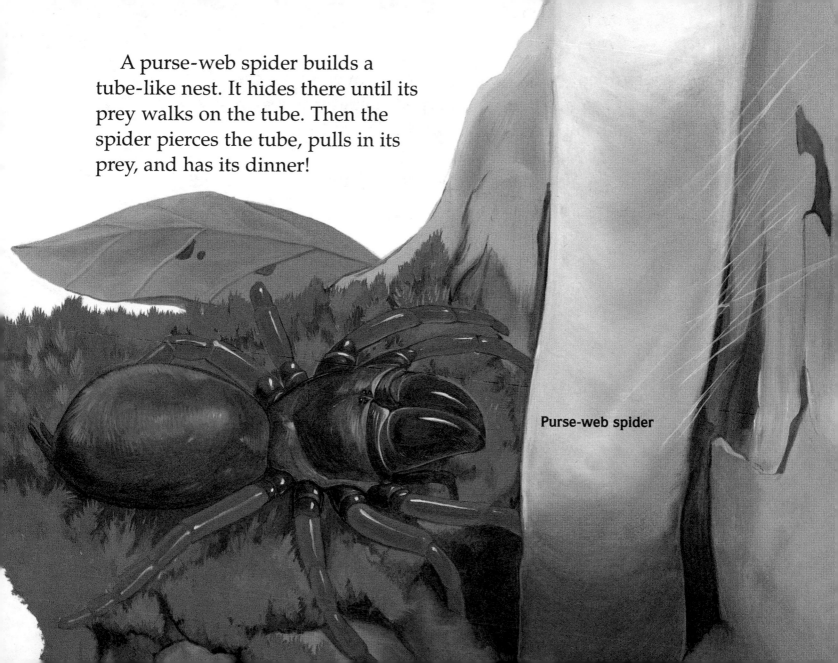

A purse-web spider builds a tube-like nest. It hides there until its prey walks on the tube. Then the spider pierces the tube, pulls in its prey, and has its dinner!

Purse-web spider

Most spiders live in webs. The webs are woven in special designs. Some of the most common types of spider webs are the orb, the funnel, and the tangled web. Each of these names describes how the web looks.

The orb web looks like a big round wheel with spokes.

Orb

Tangled

The tangled web is a jumble of silken threads, usually strung across the corner of a ceiling or wall.

The funnel is often strung among the branches of a bush or among blades of grass. It is a rounded tube that looks very much like a real funnel.

Funnel

When a web is completed for a trap, the spider covers some of the strands with sticky silk. Then the spider waits for an insect to fly into the web and become trapped.

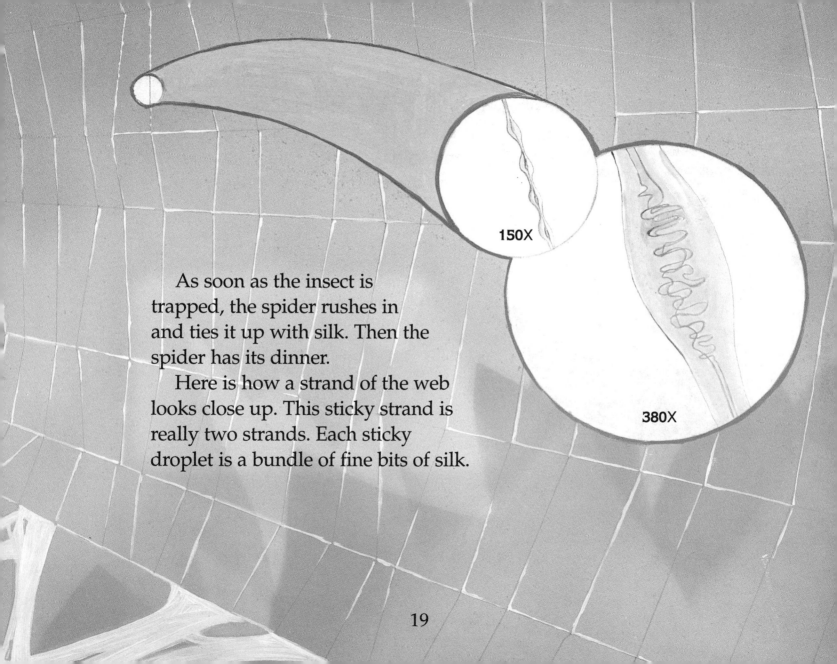

As soon as the insect is
trapped, the spider rushes in
and ties it up with silk. Then the
spider has its dinner.

Here is how a strand of the web
looks close up. This sticky strand is
really two strands. Each sticky
droplet is a bundle of fine bits of silk.

150X

380X

19

Bowl-and-doily web

You can see spider webs in many different places. Some are in trees, some are in the grass and under leaves. Some are in attics and in basements. Did you ever see a spider web in your house?

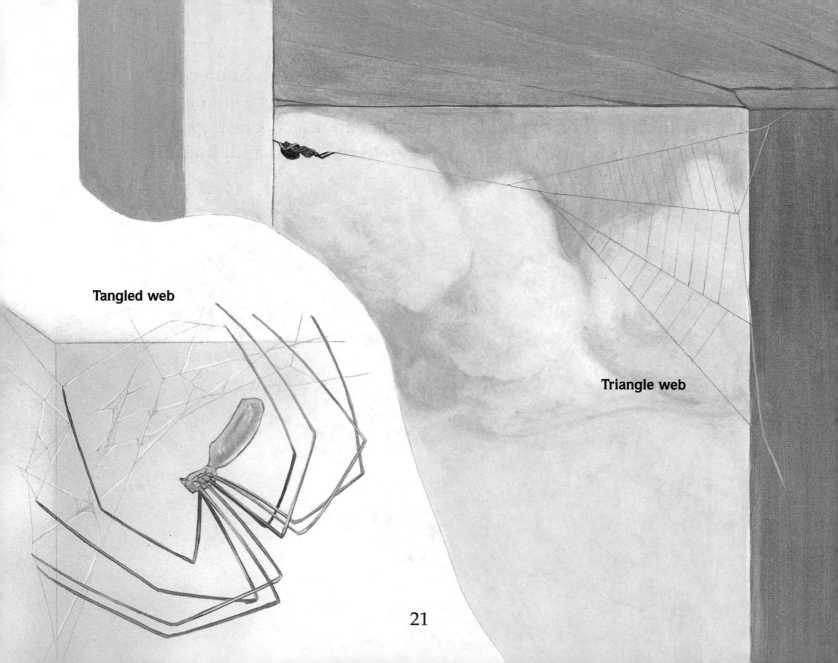

Tangled web

Triangle web

21

Not all spiders live in webs. The trapdoor spider is a hunter that lives in an underground tunnel. The door to this spider's home is lined with silk. When the spider senses that an insect is nearby, it pushes open its door. Then the spider grabs the insect and drags it back to its home.

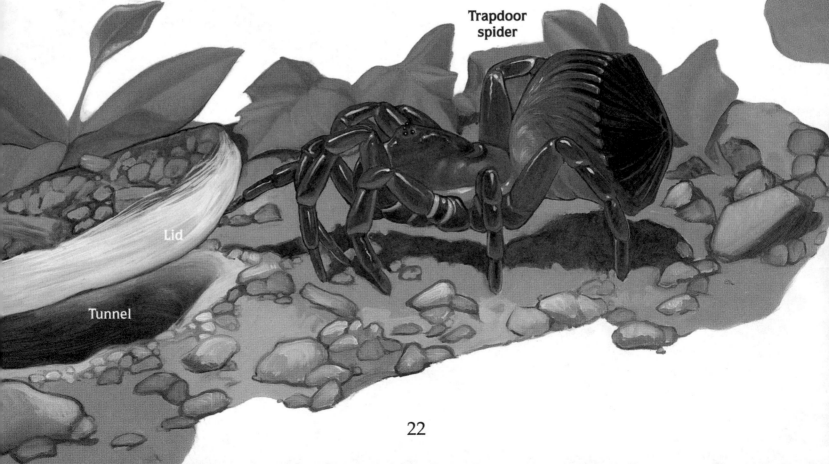

Trapdoor spider

Lid

Tunnel

The
bolas spider
captures insects
the way a cowboy
ropes a cow. The spider
spins a line of silk with a sticky
ball at the end of the line. The spider
throws out the line and "ropes" its food
by catching its victim on the sticky ball.

Bolas spider

23

Crab spider

The crab spider walks sideways just like a real crab. It lives inside flowers, where it waits to ambush insects. Most crab spiders are yellow or white. Some are able to change colors to blend in with their homes.

24

The water spider lives underwater for long periods of time. It spins a silk nest that looks like a small balloon. The spider fills the balloon with air bubbles. Then the spider can breathe underwater for several months at a time. This spider captures water insects, brings them into the bubble nest, and eats them.

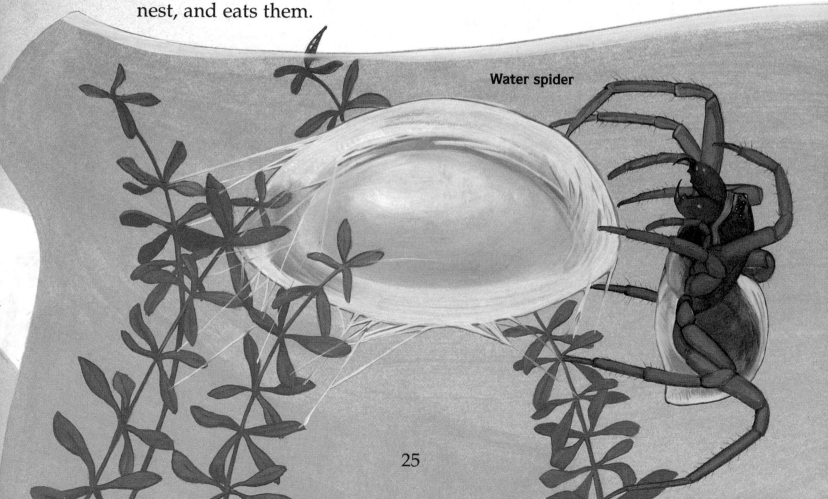

Water spider

Wolf spiders are very good hunters. Like a real wolf, this spider runs swiftly to catch its prey. Wolf spiders often live beneath rocks.

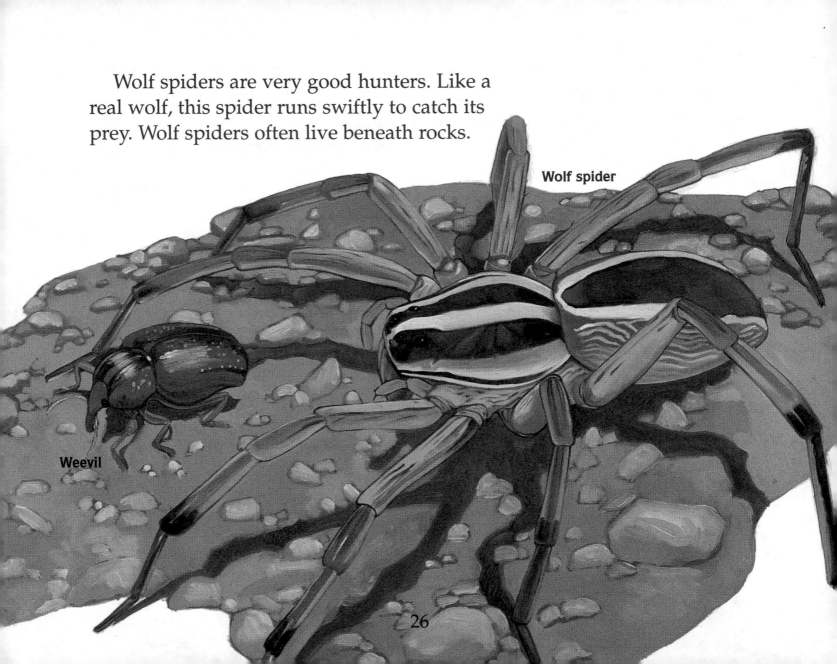

Wolf spider

Weevil

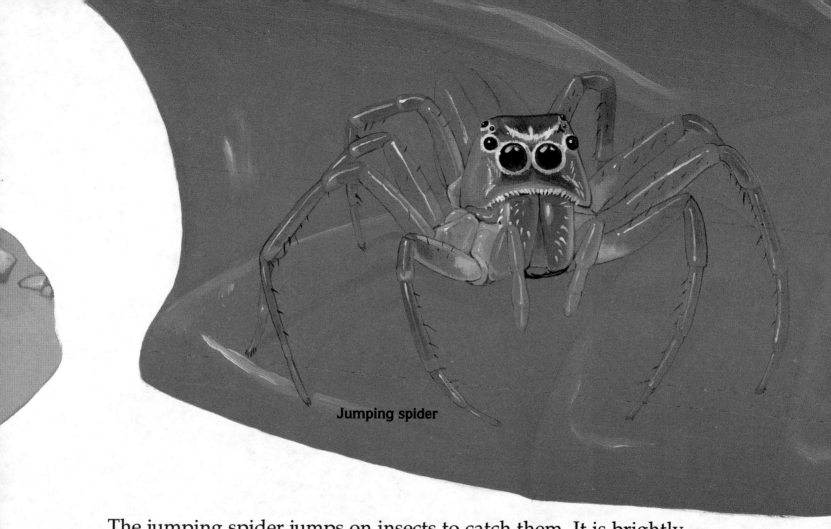

Jumping spider

The jumping spider jumps on insects to catch them. It is brightly colored and lives in warm, tropical areas. The jumping spider will let you get very close to it . . . and then it will suddenly jump away.

27

The most ferocious-looking spider of all is the tarantula (tuh-RAN-chuh-luh). This hairy hunter can be 4 to 5 inches (10 to 12 centimeters) long.

At night, the tarantula comes out of the burrow, or hole, in which it lives. The spider is ready for supper and hunts for insects, snakes, or lizards.

Tarantula

Lizard

Certain
tarantulas that
live in South America
and Australia have bites that are
poisonous to humans. Fortunately,
the tarantulas that live in the United States are not poisonous.
If you get bitten by one, it may hurt, but it will not make you sick.
Some tarantulas are so gentle that people keep them as pets.
Would you like to have a pet tarantula?

Watch out for the black widow spider.
This dangerous spider *is* poisonous. It is
easy to spot a black widow. Shiny
black in color, the black
widow has a red or yellow
mark on its abdomen.
The mark is shaped
like an hourglass.

Black widow spider

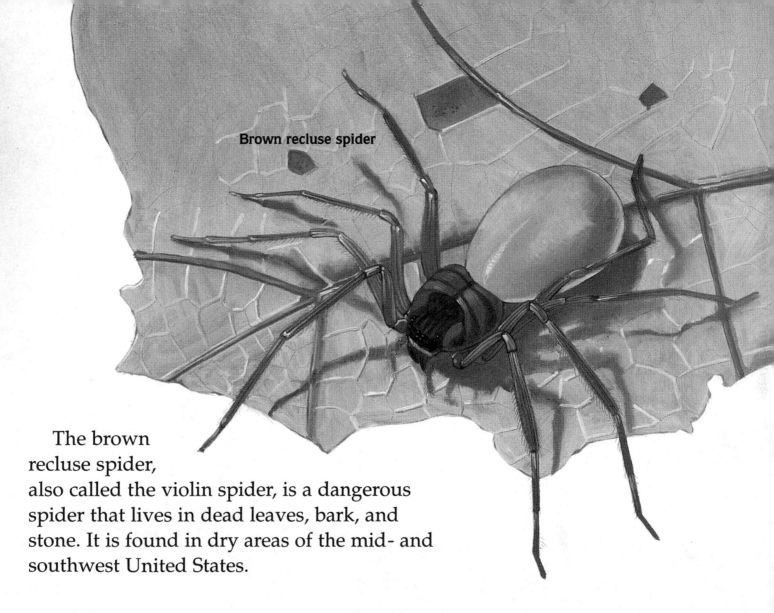

Brown recluse spider

The brown
recluse spider,
also called the violin spider, is a dangerous
spider that lives in dead leaves, bark, and
stone. It is found in dry areas of the mid- and
southwest United States.

Have you ever seen baby spiders hatching? All baby spiders hatch from eggs. The eggs are kept in a silky sac or cocoon that is spun by the mother spider.

The nursery web spider carries her egg sac under her abdomen attached to the spinnerets or in her jaws.

Nursery web spider

Egg sac

The wolf spider pulls her egg sac along behind her. The sac is attached to her spinnerets. After the babies are born, they ride on their mother's back.

Wolf spider

Babies

But most mother spiders do not take care of their babies. Because baby spiders are on their own as soon as they hatch, they must be able to spin silk right away.

The baby spins a fine silk called gossamer (GOS-uh-mer). It is very beautiful. Sometimes on a warm summer night, you can see strands of gossamer floating on the breeze.

If you see gossamer in the air, look at it closely. Baby spiders often cling to the silk and let the wind carry them long distances. This is called ballooning—and it is a quick way for a spider to travel.

34

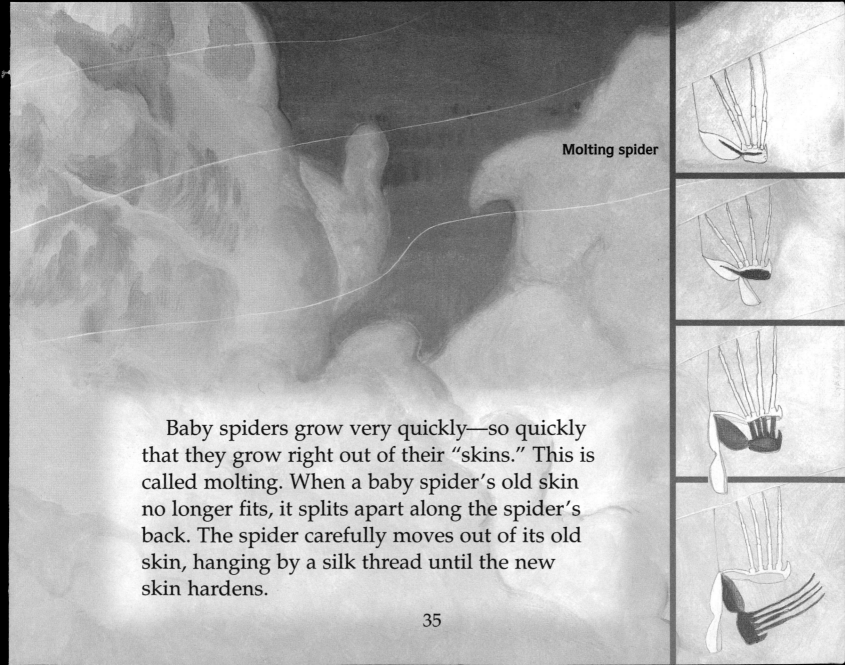

Molting spider

Baby spiders grow very quickly—so quickly that they grow right out of their "skins." This is called molting. When a baby spider's old skin no longer fits, it splits apart along the spider's back. The spider carefully moves out of its old skin, hanging by a silk thread until the new skin hardens.

Iridescent pink-toe spider

Spiders have existed on earth a long, long time. Some even lived long before the time of the dinosaurs. Scientists know of almost thirty thousand kinds of spiders, and they think there are many more yet to be discovered.

37

One reason that spiders have been able to survive successfully is because they are able to live anywhere they can find food. So the home of a spider could be a cave, a desert, a mountain, or even underwater.

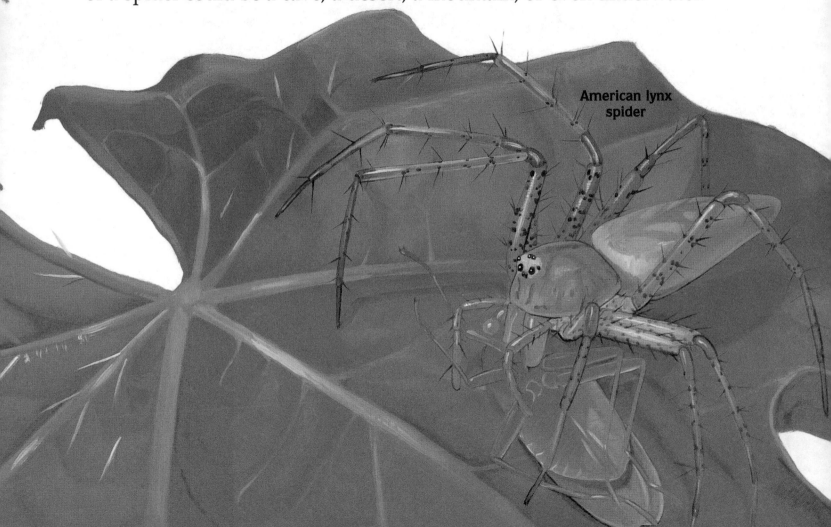

American lynx spider

Spiders are beneficial, or good, for people because they eat insects. And many insects are harmful to us because they eat the plants we grow for food.

Orb weaver

But spiders do have enemies. The spider wasp is a deadly enemy. The wasp stings the spider. Then it carries the spider back to its nest for baby wasps to feed upon.

Spider wasp

The tarantula hawk wasp preys upon female tarantulas. This deadly wasp struggles with the tarantula, then stings the spider to paralyze it. The tarantula hawk then lays an egg on the spider. When the egg hatches, the wasp larva, or baby, uses the tarantula for food.

Tarantula

Tarantula hawk wasp

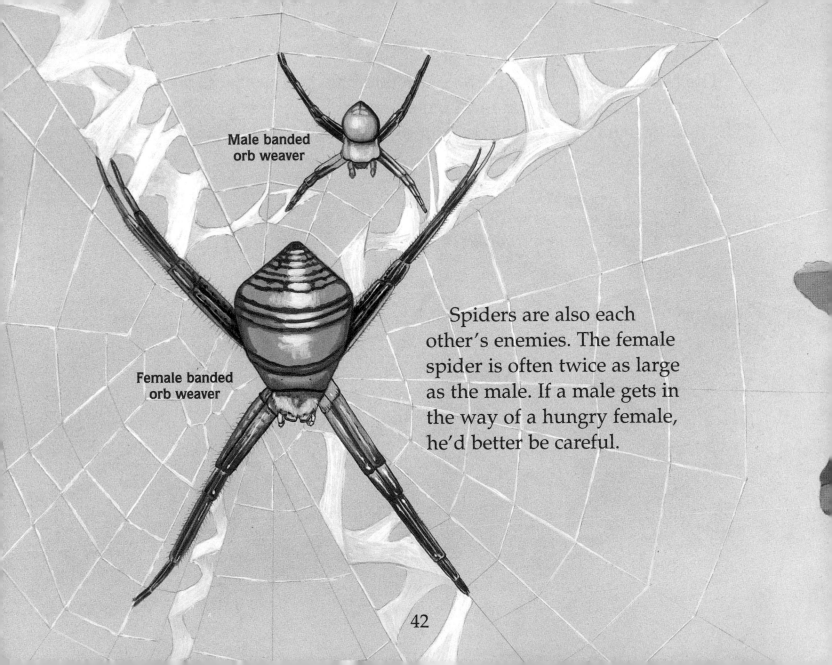

Male banded orb weaver

Female banded orb weaver

Spiders are also each other's enemies. The female spider is often twice as large as the male. If a male gets in the way of a hungry female, he'd better be careful.

Another enemy of the spider is the scorpion. The scorpion is a cousin of the spider. It is also an arachnid.

Scorpion

Desert tarantula

A scorpion looks like a small lobster. Scorpions usually hunt for food at night, when they are safe from attackers. That is when they go in search of spiders and larger insects to eat. If a scorpion senses danger, it makes a rattling sound. Then it gets ready to strike with a poisonous stinger at the end of its tail.

Asian forest scorpion

Spiders are all around us. If you look, you're sure to spot them in their webs and other places, both outdoors and indoors. Next time you see a spider, watch it closely. You may discover some fascinating secrets.

Mabel orchard spider

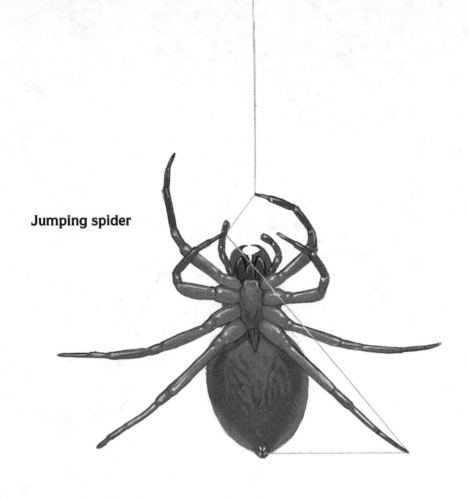

Jumping spider

For spiders play an important part in the world of nature—
a world waiting to be discovered and understood!